IGDH 7600.3
APO
MARCH 31,1993

HANDBOOK ON
FRAUD INDICATORS
FOR
CONTRACT AUDITORS

INSPECTOR GENERAL
DEPARTMENT OF DEFENSE

INSPECTOR GENERAL HANDBOOK 7600.3

HANDBOOK ON FRAUD INDICATORS
FOR CONTRACT AUDITORS

FOREWORD

This handbook is issued to increase auditor awareness of fraud indicators. While the emphasis of the handbook is toward contract auditors, the information may prove useful for all auditors. The 1988 revision to the Government Auditing Standards, issued by the Comptroller General of the United States, requires tests for compliance with applicable laws and regulations. The auditing standards require the auditor to design steps and procedures that provide a reasonable assurance of detecting errors, irregularities and illegal acts that could materially affect the financial-related audits. The 1988 revision also significantly increased the auditor's responsibility, from remaining alert for fraud indicators to designing steps to reasonably assure detecting irregularities and illegal acts.

Previously, three separate handbooks were issued on fraud indicators and scenarios. The first, Handbook on Labor Fraud Indicators, was issued in August 1985; the second, Handbook on Fraud Indicators: Material, was issued July 1986; and the third, Handbook on Scenarios of Potential Defective Pricing Fraud, was issued December 1986. This update incorporates the information in one handbook, eliminates duplicate scenarios and provides additional information to help auditors recognize fraud indicators. The scenarios are arranged by three major groupings of audits-incurred cost, forward pricing and defective pricing. Many of the scenarios and fraud indicators are applicable to other audits besides the ones that are identified within this handbook.

A handbook on the Role of the Contract Auditor in a Criminal Investigation, IGDH 7600.2, has also been issued. The handbook contains insights and guidelines on the auditor's role in the fraud investigation. Numerous other guides are available on the auditor's roles and responsibilities.

This handbook compiles fraud indicators related to some common fraud schemes and other sensitive audits. The various scenarios describe situations when auditors should make a fraud referral. Our intent is to build on the auditor's knowledge and raise the awareness level sufficient to identify fraud indicators and make the referrals, where necessary. Designing audits to find fraud indicators and recognizing those indicators requires creativity and knowledge, along with a common sense level of professional skepticism and suspicion. Approaching each audit with fraud indicators in mind provides the auditor with the proper alertness and awareness needed to assess the different situations.

Auditors are not responsible for proving fraud. This is the job of the investigator. Finding and reporting fraud indicators are an auditor's responsibility and he/she should "think fraud" when performing a review. This awareness factor cannot be overemphasized. In cases where a Government official or agency may appear to have approved a suspected irregularity or illegal act, the auditor is still responsible for making a referral. The key issue is whether the auditor would have referred the suspected irregularity if the government official(s) or agency had not acted.

On the other hand, an auditor must not automatically conclude that every contractor commits fraudulent acts or that every fraud indicator denotes fraud. By looking for fraud indicators and properly assessing them during an audit, the auditor is taking the proper approach to uncovering fraudulent acts and, thereby, protecting the Government's interests. We anticipate that the publication of this handbook will help auditors use their intuitive and professional judgment, creativity, imagination and technical skills to identify potential fraudulent schemes.

(signed)
Derek J. Vander Schaaf
Deputy Inspector General

HANDBOOK ON FRAUD INDICATORS
FOR CONTRACT AUDITORS

CONTENTS

I. FRAUD DETECTION OVERVIEW

In order to properly identify fraud indicators, the auditor must remember the environment in which fraud may occur. The conditions can be summarized in two words-opportunity and motive. The factors apply separately and jointly to individuals and the company. Much emphasis is given to individuals committing fraud against organizations for personal benefit; however, the contract auditor will mostly deal with organizational fraud-fraud committed for the direct benefit of the organization and, therefore, the indirect benefit of the individual. Auditors should remember that individuals who commit organizational fraud may be motivated differently than when they directly benefit. In the case of organizational fraud, the individual benefits through bonuses, raises, promotions or job retention. A more subtle motivation relates to increased self-esteem or co-worker/supervisor praise or envy.

Various accounting/auditing associations have issued auditing standards related to fraud detection and assessment of internal controls. While Government contract auditors are required to comply with the Government Auditing Standards issued by the Comptroller General, other auditing standards provide insight into how to identify appropriate fraud indicators. The Government Auditing Standards also incorporate the American Institute of Certified Public Accountants auditing standards for field work and reporting for financial audits. According to Chapter Two, "Types of Government Audits," financial- related audits may include audits of contracts (i.e., bid proposals, contract pricing, amounts billed, amounts due on termination claims, compliance with contract terms), internal control systems and structure over accounting, financial reporting and transaction processing, financial systems or fraud.

The auditor should know the contractor and have a thorough understanding of the company's internal controls. The contractor is responsible for establishing and maintaining an effective system of internal controls that safeguards the assets of the company and assures the reliability of its financial records. Weaknesses, breakdowns or circumventions of the internal controls create opportunities that may result in fraudulent practices.

The auditor must always remember that fraud indicators are only symptoms or characteristics of possible fraud. An indicator may be caused by the fraudulent act itself or may result from an attempt to hide the fraudulent scheme. In addition, the auditor must consider the total picture when deciding whether to refer a suspected irregularity. Some indicators, such as a falsified or phony document, may be, in and of themselves, enough to trigger a referral. In other cases, the auditor may need to recognize the interrelationship of several seemingly unrelated deficiencies or indicators, which when combined, warrant a referral. The auditor must be careful that while determining whether to refer a situation or not, he/she is not attempting to determine criminal intent. The auditor is not responsible for establishing that a contractor's actions were intentionally taken in an effort to deceive the Government as part of a scheme to commit a fraudulent act. That is the job of the investigator and the prosecutor.

While the scenarios in this handbook are organized by the three broad types of audits, many of the fraud indicators described in the scenarios may be found in any type of audit. Auditors should familiarize themselves with the basic knowledge provided by the scenarios and creatively use it while performing any audit or review.

II. INCURRED COST AUDITS

INTRODUCTION

Incurred cost audits include the audit of direct and indirect costs claimed by contractors. The audit objective is to determine if the claimed costs are reasonable, allocable to the contract, in compliance with generally accepted accounting principles and Cost Accounting Standards, and not prohibited by the contract, Government statute or regulation. There are numerous schemes and scenarios that may occur in any element of direct or indirect cost; therefore, the auditor must be knowledgeable and alert for fraud indicators when performing the many different incurred cost audits.

In the past, the highest number of fraud referrals have been found in incurred cost-type audits. Proper risk assessment combined with transaction testing and verification to source documents provides greater opportunity to detect fraud indicators. Many of the following fraud indicators may be identified while performing other audits. The auditor must recognize the effect mischarging may have on preaward and postaward audits.

---

1. LABOR COSTS

Labor, direct and indirect, can be the most significant cost charged to Government contracts. Generally, it is the most difficult area to review. The critical issue is whether the employee's time is properly charged to the project actually worked on. No third party documentation exists such as invoices, purchase orders, etc., to support labor cost. Without any external independent or physical verification, labor is very vulnerable to manipulation. The most important control in the labor accounting system is the individual employee and the employee's acceptance of the responsibility to accurately record time worked.

Therefore, the auditor must know and understand the contractor's labor accounting system in order to properly assess the adequacy of the contractor's internal controls, design appropriate audit steps and properly analyze the information gathered. Another key element in every labor review is the proper assessment of the Government's risk and vulnerability. The auditor should perform a preliminary analysis to determine the appropriate combination of labor audit techniques required.

There are two audit approaches for evaluating labor charging-comprehensive and traditional. Comprehensive audit techniques focus on a preinterview analysis of labor charging patterns and employee interviews. Traditional audit techniques include labor reconciliations employee floor-checks. As the term implies, comprehensive audit techniques are generally more extensive than traditional audit techniques. The employee interview covers a specific time period and focuses on a labor charging pattern. Whereas, the traditional floorcheck is used primarily to verify, at any given time, that selected employees' labor costs are being properly charged to the work actually being performed. An audit may incorporate a combination of the two audit techniques based on the auditor's assessment of the risk areas. However, information gathered during a traditional floorcheck may prompt an adjustment to the audit scope to include a more comprehensive approach to labor charging. The floorcheck and the interview test the adequacy of internal controls on labor recording.

II. INCURRED COST AUDITS

To be effective, floorchecks and interviews should be conducted at the employee's work station. Supporting documentation, such as work orders, employee time logs, notes or letters, should be obtained for any potential audit findings disclosed during the interview. Also, an interview should never be conducted without adequate preinterview analysis. The auditor should use all available information to plan and perform the labor review.

a. Direct and Indirect Labor

The Scenario

The auditor was assigned to review the labor costs at a medium-sized contractor. The contractor had a mix of Government cost-type and fixed-price contracts and some commercial work. First, the auditor computed the percentage of direct to indirect labor costs and compared it to prior year ratios. Then the auditor compared the indirect labor account totals from the prior year to the current year and noted the percentage change. The auditor also computed the percentage of total direct labor charged to each contract/work order to determine which charge numbers had the highest percentage of direct labor charges. The auditor noted the following:

-Total indirect labor costs increased 30 percent from the previous year.

-Total direct labor costs increased 15 percent from the previous year.

-Indirect labor identified as Engineering Development increased by 15 percent over the previous year.

-Bid and Proposal (B&P) and Independent Research and Development {IR&D) costs exceeded the ceiling amount by 10 percent.

-Direct labor costs on certain fixed-price production contracts decreased by 30 percent.

-Direct labor costs on the Government cost-type contracts increased by 20 percent.

-Direct labor costs charged to commercial contracts increased by roughly 5 percent over the previous year.

The auditor noted that many of the decreases and increases were not readily explainable; therefore, the auditor computed the same percentages for direct and indirect labor by quarter. Next, the auditor analyzed the quarterly charges to determine if any shifts in charging patterns existed. The auditor found the following patterns:

-Charges to B&P and IR&D dropped off sharply in the third quarter. For the fourth quarter, only insignificant amounts were charged to those accounts.

-Charges to cost-type contracts increased sharply in the third quarter and stayed high in the fourth quarter.

-Charges to commercial contracts and Engineering Development were consistent over all four quarters.

-Charges to fixed-price production contracts started decreasing in the second quarter and continued decreasing throughout the last two quarters.

The auditor then selected individuals to interview who had changed their charging patterns during the year, researched the contracts/projects involved and designed the appropriate interview questions for each employee. The auditor also analyzed the contractor's sales and reviewed the headcounts. After reviewing the information gathered during the process, the auditor summarized everything he/she learned:

-The contractor had opened a new manufacturing plant in Mexico and assigned the majority of the fixed-price production work to that plant. The new plant had been planned for at least a year but was never discussed with the Government representatives.

-The commercial contracts were for product lines still in the late development/early production stage. Several of the products were experiencing performance problems which indicated additional engineering services were needed. Engineers working on solving the problems were charging their time to Engineering Development.

-Employees who had been working mostly on B&P and IR&D projects for the first half of the year had been instructed to stop charging those accounts in the third quarter. Instead they were given blank time cards to sign at the beginning of the week to simplify preparation of time cards. They were also provided new project numbers to charge even though they were still performing the same work. The new project numbers turned out to represent cost-type contracts.

General Comments. Improper charging of costs is the most common fraud indicator that auditors have found and referred for investigation. Improper charging of costs can occur for numerous reasons, such as wrong charge numbers and misunderstandings. Auditors should always request a complete explanation for discrepancies between what the employee says he/she is working on, what he/she is charging, and what the contractor's established accounting policies and procedures are. The auditor should theft fully evaluate the contractor's rationale and determine its validity before accepting or rejecting the costs.

Note. Section 824 of the National Defense Authorization Act for Fiscal Year 1991 (public Law 101-510) and Section 802 of the National Defense Authorization Act for Fiscal Years 1992 and 1993 (public Law 102-190) revised Federal Acquisition Regulation (FAR) 31.205.18, Independent Research and Development and Bid and Proposal Costs. Some of the more significant changes follow:

-Effective for contractor fiscal years beginning on or after October 1, 1992, the requirement for negotiation of advance agreements no longer exists.

-The formula method for establishing IR&D and B&P ceilings for companies not required to negotiate advance agreements is also eliminated. The IR&D/B&P costs for those companies are allowable to the extent they are allocable and reasonable.

-For major contractors, effective for fiscal years (FYs) beginning on or after October 1, 1992, IR&D/B&P costs are allowable as indirect expenses on contracts to the extent they are allocable and reasonable. However, for a 3-year transition period (FYs 1993-1995), a limitation was instituted on the allowable general increase in IR&D/B&P costs per year. The limitation is based on the prior year's allowable costs (the lower of the ceiling amount or the actual allowable costs incurred) adjusted for inflation plus a 5-percent increase.

Therefore, even though the method for calculating the ceiling amount has been changed, sufficient opportunity and motivation still exists for cost mischarging. The auditor must remain alert for instances when the contractor improperly charges costs to obtain the maximum reimbursement of those costs.

FRAUD INDICATORS

- **Distinctive charging patterns.**

- **Sudden, significant shifts in charging.**

- **Decrease in charges to projects/contracts in overrun or near ceilings.**

- **A disproportionate percentage of employees charging indirect.**

- **Large number of employees reclassified from direct to indirect or vice versa.**

- **Same employees constantly reclassified from direct to indirect or vice versa.**

- **Weak internal controls over labor charging, such as employee time cards signed in advance, employee time cards filled in by the supervisor, time cards filled in pencil, or time cards filled in at the end of the pay period.**

- **Actual hours and dollars consistently at or near budgeted amounts.**

- **Use of adjusting journal entries to shift costs between contracts, IR&D, B&P, commercial work.**

- **Significant increases or decreases in charging to sensitive accounts.**

- **Employee's time charged differently than associated travel costs.**

---

b. Uncompensated Overtime

The Scenario

While performing a floorcheck of salaried employees, the auditor noted that almost every employee stated that he or she traditionally worked more than 40 hours a week but only recorded 40 hours on the time card. The employees were not given informal credit for the extra hours, such as additional time off. The employees also stated that supervisors specifically instructed them not to record the extra hours in spite of the company's policies. The auditor then performed floorchecks to determine what projects the employees were working on after normal work hours. Generally, the employees were working on Government fixed-price contracts or commercial contracts. The auditor also found certain employees working on a cost-type contract that was overrun and behind schedule. Based on the information gathered during the floorchecks, the auditor estimated that the amount of unpaid overtime was approximately 20 hours a week equating annually to roughly $20,000 an employee. The auditor determined those figures were significant for the size of the company. The auditor then reviewed the contractor's accounting policies and procedures and verified that the contractor's policy was to account for all hours worked and charge the employee's salary accordingly.

General Comments. Uncompensated overtime is hours worked in excess of 8 hours a day or 40 hours per week by salaried employees who are paid a fixed amount per week, month or year regardless of the number of hours worked. Salaried employees are generally exempt from the Fair Labor Standards Act (FLSA) because their rate of pay exceeds a threshold below which the payment of overtime for hours worked in excess of 8 a day or 40 per week is required. The FLSA recognizes a cutoff at which employees no longer require the protection of law from working overtime without pay because they are adequately paid for their services. Therefore, "uncompensated overtime" or "unpaid overtime " are really misnomers since the salaries of exempt employees under the FLSA are considered compensation for all hours worked. Also, because of the added responsibilities of their jobs, salaried employees are usually paid significantly higher wages than hourly employees. Nearly every segment of the United States society has professional salaried employees who work uncompensated overtime. However, an inequity in the costing of Government contracts may occur if uncompensated overtime is worked, but not accounted for, and more than one contract or project is worked on by the salaried employee. The lack of proper accounting for the overtime hours can create the potential for the manipulation of the contractor's labor accounting system.

If the auditor identifies a situation where the contractor refuses to record all hours worked by exempt employees, he/she should expand the floorchecks or employee interviews to determine whether the failure of the contractor to record all time worked results in a material difference in the charging of costs. Uncompensated overtime can increase contractor profits, especially on a fixed-price contract which was bid on the basis of a 40-hour week and employees are either required to work uncompensated overtime or they voluntarily do so. Contractor profits increase because for every additional uncompensated overtime hour per week an employee works, a lower effective hourly rate is paid by the contractor. That practice can also cause problems if the contractor wishes to use history to bid follow-on contracts. Those fraud indicators may also be found while performing a compliance review with FAR 31.201.4, Determining Allocability and Cost Accounting Standard (CAS) 418, Allocation of Direct and Indirect Cost.

FRAUD INDICATORS

- **Professional staff required to work a significant amount of unpaid overtime on a variety of projects-both direct and indirect.**

- **Salaried employees only charging the first 8 hours worked during any day for an extended period.**

- **A pattern of management directed unpaid overtime with employee bonus based on the extra hours worked.**

- **Cost-type Government contracts worked during the first 8 hours and fixed price or commercial contract work performed only during the unpaid hours.**

- **Overrun contracts/projects worked on only during unpaid hours.**

- **Encouraging employees to work significant unpaid overtime but to not record the hours in direct conflict with company policy.**

---

c.   Other Schemes Involving Labor Costs

Program Management Costs

The inconsistent treatment of program management costs is usually thought of as an accounting system inadequacy, but auditors should not overlook the possibility of fraud. When the auditor finds managers charged indirect on fixed-price and commercial contracts and finds managers charged direct on cost-type contracts, he/she must gather additional information to analyze that fraud indicator further. Fraud indicators could be identified from a number of ways that costs are charged. Knowledge of contractor estimating and charging practices, policies and procedures is essential to recognizing fraud indicators.

Contract Development Type Contracts

Mischarging of labor costs on contract development-type contracts is another high-risk area. During the design phase of a new program, the Government may award a number of contracts to competing contractors. At the completion of the development contracts, the contractor with the best product at the best price may be awarded the long-term production contract. Since the emphasis is on building the best product, the incentive is to devote all possible resources during the development phase. At the same time, cost is also a critical factor. How can that paradox be resolved? The auditor may find mischarging of direct labor to indirect accounts such as engineering design and development effort, contractor-sponsored IR&D projects that could be reallocated to overhead or General and Administrative (G&A) accounts, or any other contracts where the costs could be billed without being noticed. The incentive to hold down costs is great, increasing the Government's vulnerability to mischarging.

---

2. MATERIAL COSTS

Material includes raw material, purchased parts, subcontracts and intercompany transfers. The cost of material is usually charged direct to a contract. In some instances, material cost can be accumulated in a pool and allocated as a direct charge.

Material cost reviews concentrate on proper charging and reasonableness of cost. Proper charging is based on the material requirements for the item being procured. The reasonableness of the cost depends, to a large extent, on the contractor's material accounting and related systems. Material cost audits involve reviewing the internal controls and the contractor's purchasing, receiving and inventory systems. The auditor also must review the contractor's material requirements system to verify its accuracy.

Material is a high-risk area because it is susceptible to physical loss and requires detailed analysis and review. Evaluating proposed versus actual material requirements and standards plus performing a physical verification of material use requires technical assistance and auditor initiative.

Subcontracts make up a large percentage of contractor proposed material costs and are particularly vulnerable to fraud. Contractors may employ a multitude of schemes or just one to improperly bid subcontract costs. A subcontract management audit provides a thorough review of the basis for those costs. Proposal and postaward audit reviews may provide leads and indicators in the subcontract area, but most audits do not review the root causes of the fraud indicators.

Past congressional hearings have focused on abuses in subcontract management, specifically subcontractor kickbacks. Estimates were that from 10 to 50 percent of all subcontractors or vendors were involved in some type of payment scheme. The abuses could range from paying for a buyer's lunch to payoffs in the thousands of dollars. Since materials comprise a large part of all major DoD procurements, kickbacks/bribes add substantial sums to the price of everything the Government buys.

Buyers can easily disguise kickbacks/bribes schemes by producing documentation to justify the award of a purchase order or subcontract. Kickbacks/bribes occur most frequently in subcontracts under $100,000. Purchase orders under $10,000 are extremely vulnerable because of lack of scrutiny.

Kickback/bribery schemes are arrangements between vendors and the prime contractor's buyers, high-level officials or even owners. The vendor agrees to pay back those individuals a percentage of all subcontracts it is awarded by the prime. One kickback scheme is called a "bump" agreement. In those cases, the prime's agent tells the vendor's employees how much he/she can raise the bid and still be low bidder. Another system is complementary bidding. Complementary bidding revolves around various vendors taking turns being the low bidder. When a company is not designated the low bidder, it submits an artificially high bid to protect the designated vendor's bid. In other instances, the prime contractor's agent may disclose the legitimate bids to the designated vendor so he/she can underbid the competition. The prime contractor's representative may also disqualify legitimate low bids on the basis of technical or financial capability and award the order to the preferred vendor. Some of these schemes may also indicate a potential anti-trust violation.

Kickbacks/bribes can be in various forms. Cash, illegal drugs, cars, appliances, tolls, airline tickets and package vacations have all been used as payoffs. In some extreme cases, the recipient of the kickback has sent bills to the vendor for purchased items or used the vendor's credit cards for purchases.

The vendor could also pay kickbacks to a nonexistent company or one that is created solely to facilitate payments from the vendor to the recipient of the kickback. Those payments may be for consulting services or services and materials that appear related to the contract; however, when compared to overall costs and other actual charges, they show up as unusual.

Standard audit approaches and contractor purchasing system reviews are not likely to uncover kickbacks/bribes. The documentation in the vendor files may appear legitimate and invoices usually do not reflect the kickbacks/bribes. Instead, internal control reviews should be used to assess the contractor's vulnerability in those areas. The contractor's failure to monitor and control its employees' activities contributes to the problem through lack of attention and inaction.

a. Material Transfers -Material Requirements System

The Scenario

While performing an internal control review of the material requirements system, the auditor noted an extremely large number of transfers between work orders. Recognizing that that may be a significant weakness in the contractor's system and a fraud indicator, the auditor expanded the scope of the review. Initial questioning of contractor personnel-the controller and the inventory/stores manager-indicated that the company's material requirements system was designed to transfer parts based on prioritized needs. For that reason, the company personnel dismissed the auditor's concern about the large number of transfers. "The system is merely operating as it was set up to do," the auditor was told. When a higher priority work order was set up, the system transferred existing parts to it from other lower priority work orders. Parts reordered for the lower priority work orders were charged the new (usually higher) prices, while the higher priority work order was charged the existing {usually lower) price. The auditor then reviewed the delivery schedules for the various work orders to determine the accuracy of the assigned priorities. The auditor found that the higher priority work orders were generally commercial or firm fixed price work. The lower priority work was generally fixed price incentive work. Another additional factor reviewed was the contractor's cost performance on the various work orders. The higher priority work was also closer to or over budget than the lower priority work. The delivery schedule had no specific relationship to the priority set.

General Comments. Continuous internal controls and system reviews are an integral part of auditing any company. If the integrity of the company's accounting and related operating systems cannot be relied on, the auditor cannot rely on the information generated. Each system's integrity must be continually reviewed and verified. Any transfer of material costs must be reviewed for appropriateness.

FRAUD INDICATORS

- **Transfers from ongoing jobs to open work orders for items previously delivered.**

- **Transfers from ongoing jobs to open work orders for items scheduled for delivery in the distant future.**

- **Transfers from Government contracts (job orders) to commercial job orders.**

- **Transfers from cost-type job orders to fixed-price job orders.**

- **Transfers at costs substantially different (higher or lower) than actual.**

- **Mass transfers from one job order to various other job orders. No physical inventory is left on the original job order, but it still has costs charged to.**

---

b. Subcontractor/Vendor Kickbacks

The Scenario

The auditor was assigned an incurred cost audit at a nonmajor contractor. The contractor had a mix of commercial, fixed-price and cost-type contracts and subcontracts. The auditor selected several sensitive indirect accounts to review and statistically selected transactions for testing. The sample items were traced back to source documents to determine the allowability, allocability and reasonableness of the costs. The auditor reviewed several items charged to the "Business meals" account and noted the items were not properly documented. The names of the individuals were noted but the reason for the meeting/meal was not recorded. The auditor discussed the documentation with the contractor representative who stated that the individuals involved worked for one of their major customers-a DoD prime contractor. The auditor decided to expand the review of the account. The auditor found that approximately 50 percent of the charges were not properly documented. The auditor also noted that the same individuals were having their lunches and dinners paid for on a continuous basis. The auditor decided to review the company's voluntary deletions very closely. The auditor found indications that items such as carpeting and vacation packages had been purchased for the prime contractor's employees. The auditor referred the matter to the appropriate investigative organization and notified in writing the audit office cognizant of the prime contractor.

General Comments. Detection of vendor kickbacks is difficult. Standard audit procedures normally will not uncover such schemes. The auditor must be alert to obvious weaknesses in the contractor's internal controls that make taking payoffs easy. Audits of the prime contractor's material purchasing, receiving and storing systems will point out other weaknesses or noncompliance with existing contractor policies and procedures. Physical verification of the existence of inventories or materials charged direct to a job will also show how vulnerable the contractor's system is to fraud. A subcontract management review may be the best way to evaluate the prime contractor's policies and procedures for awarding orders to vendors to assure that proper procedures are followed.

FRAUD INDICATORS

- **Poor contractor internal controls over key functional areas, such as purchasing, receiving and storing.**

- **Lack of separation of duties between purchasing and receiving.**

- **Lack of separation of duties in the purchasing department. Buyers should be rotated to prevent familiarity with specific vendors.**

- **None of few contractor policies on ethical business practices.**

- **Poor enforcement of existing contractor policies on conflicts of interest or acceptance of gratuities.**

- **Purchasing employees maintaining a standard of living obviously exceeding their income.**

- **Instances of buyers or other employees circumventing established contractor procedures for competition of subcontracts.**

- **Poor or no established contractor procedures for competition of subcontracts.**

- **Poor documentation supporting award of subcontracts.**

- **Lack of competitive awards.**

- **Nonaward of subcontract to lowest bidder.**

- **A one-time payment for services or materials usually bought from another vender(s). The kickback recipient could be using the company to obtain his payoff.**

---

3. INDIRECT COSTS

An indirect cost is any cost that is not directly identified with a single final cost objective, but is identified with two or more final cost objectives or an intermediate cost objective. Indirect costs are incurred as a result of business decisions made at all levels of management. Those decisions may be based on established policies or may be a manager's choice among several options for achieving an objective. To be allowable, indirect costs must be allowable, allocable and reasonable.

IGDH 7600.3

Beginning in March 1985, DoD contractors were required to certify, in accordance with Public Law 99-145, that all costs included in a claim to establish billing or final indirect cost rates are allowable in accordance with contract requirements and DoD cost principles. Since enactment of the certification requirements, Contractors have spent more time reviewing indirect expenses and voluntarily deleting unallowable items from their claims for payment and indirect cost submissions.

a. Adjusting Journal Entries-Labor Transfers

The Scenario

During the monthly review of the contractor's adjusting journal entries, the auditor noted transfers from a number of work orders to other work orders or overhead accounts. Recognizing that as a fraud indicator, the auditor expanded the scope of review. The auditor requested the supporting documentation for the entries and learned which employee labor charges had been transferred, the rationale behind the transfers and the responsible individuals. The journal entry explanation was "Charged wrong work order." Labor costs were transferred from B&P projects and a large cost-type Government contract. The costs were charged to a number of cost-type Government contracts and an overhead account. Additional research disclosed that the large cost-type contract was for a major weapon system and, therefore, was subject to Cost Schedule Control System Criteria (C/SCSC). Interviews with the responsible individuals-the controller and program managers-disclosed two important facts:

-The B&P pool had recently reached the ceiling negotiated in the advance agreement.

-Work completed under the C/SCSC-covered contract was behind schedule and labor costs were over budget. The estimate at completion did not reflect the problems and the variance analysis did not offer any corrective action plans to get on schedule or within the budget.

Additional transfers were later found from the B&P account and the C/SCSC contract to an overhead account for warranty/rework. The other cost-type contracts which had previously received transfers were near their funding ceiling.

General Comments. Transfers of costs are always suspect. The auditor should always obtain a sufficient explanation for transfers and expand the scope of audit to adequately review and evaluate the contractor's rationale. In most cases, the auditor cannot accept the contractor's explanation without some additional audit work. At major contractor locations, the auditor should review the adjusting journal entries on a monthly basis and pay special attention to cost transfers. The auditor must also be skeptical when costs are transferred between contract line items. Some contracts include different types of reimbursements or fundings. The auditor should always determine the nature of the work orders/charge numbers involved in the transfers and determine what motive the contractor would have for the cost transfers. That is not to say most transfers are unacceptable-just that transfers are an easy way to move costs and thus highly sensitive to manipulation. Therefore, close scrutiny is required before accepting any cost transfer.

FRAUD INDICATORS

- **Transfers from IR&D and B&P accounts.**

- **Transfers from fixed-price Government or commercial contracts.**

- **Transfers from or to cost-type Government contracts.**

- **Transfers from or to indirect accounts.**

- **Transfers to any type of holding or suspense account.**

- **Transfers from one contract line item or work order to another line item or work order on the same contract but with different appropriations.**

---

b. Review of Sensitive Accounts

The Scenario

During the review of the contractor's overhead submission, the auditor noted a sharp increase in the inventory write-off (obsolescence) account costs in comparison to the total direct material costs. Examination of the purchase order history disclosed that identical parts were being purchased during the same timeframe they were written off the inventory as obsolete. Further examination disclosed the company was purchasing the parts from the same company it had sold the "obsolete" parts to. The auditor checked with the company controller and discovered:

> -Parts being written off as obsolete/scrap were not necessarily excess to the company's needs.

> -The parts were not really being "scrapped." They were being sold to a warehousing service firm for nominal prices.

> -When the company reacquired the part, it paid a substantially higher price based on a preestablished formula.
> -Parts were written off as excess and sold to a warehousing firm and shortly thereafter were repurchased from the warehousing firm for contracts.

> -The company was the only party eligible to "buy" (reacquire) the parts it "sold" to the servicing firm. The company was provided a monthly listing of all its inventory being stored by the servicing firm.

General Comments. Monitoring charges to sensitive accounts must be done on an ongoing basis. Charges to an inventory write-off or a scrap account should be reviewed since they represent an easy way to mischarge costs. In addition, improperly "scrapped" parts can be personal gain to company employees. Employees may arrange the sale of valuable items to associates for resale. Continuous purchases of items written off as scrap, obsolete or excess may also indicate a kickback or bribery scheme. The auditor must thoroughly understand the company's policies, procedures and internal

---

Controls governing obsolete or scrap material. The auditor must also know the applicable Government procurement regulations, cost accounting standards and contract clauses.

FRAUD INDICATORS

- **Significant increases or decreases to a sensitive account, such as scrap, rework, inventory write-off or rework.**

- **Recent purchases of items written off as scrap, obsolete or excess, especially from the same vendors.**

- **Repurchasing the same items written off as scrap, obsolete or excess from the buyer of the items.**

---

c. Review of Consulting/Professional Service Accounts

The Scenario

The auditor was assigned the task of reviewing the indirect cost accounts for the contractor's FY 1990 submission. The first audit steps performed were a nomenclature review and comparative analysis with the prior year audited costs. The auditor then selected certain sensitive accounts to review in detail. One obvious selection was consulting costs due to the inclusion of potentially unallowable costs. In addition, the claimed consulting costs had increased by a higher percentage than the other accounts. The auditor initially selected a judgmental sample and requested the supporting documentation from the contractor. Of the 10 items selected for review, the auditor found the following:

> -Three were properly supported with detailed consulting agreements, invoices and reports. The subjects covered were germane to the contractor's operations and provided appropriate recommendations to improve the efficiency of certain operations. The contractor implemented the majority of the recommendations.

> -Five were for retainer fees. Two were for law firms the contractor had used extensively during each of the past 3 years for various legal matters, which were considered allowable. The applicable agreements contained the necessary level of detail and the fees were considered reasonable. Three were for companies whose services were not previously used. The retainer agreements were not specific in what services the companies were to provide; however, they did detail who would perform the services and the hourly rate involved. The services, as described, appeared to be for marketing. The individuals' resumes were not available. The retainer fees were higher for those firms than the law firms. The company representative could not explain the higher fees or the specifics of what services were to be provided.

> -Two were invoices from the above-mentioned "marketing" firms for services rendered in addition to the retainer fees. The invoices were vague in describing services rendered and only referred to the retainer agreement. The expense was a lump sum with no breakdown of hours expended, hourly rate, travel expenses or other expenses. No trip reports or other summary reports were available.

The auditor asked for additional information on the three "marketing" firms; however, the contractor was unable to provide anything other than verbal assurances of the services provided.

The auditor noted that the invoices showed a post office box as a mailing address. The auditor looked and found no listing of the firms in the telephone directory.

FRAUD INDICATORS

- **No formal signed agreements or contracts; however, large sums paid for "services rendered" based on invoices with few specifics.**

- **Formal agreements or contracts exist but are vague as to services to be rendered, and no other documented support, such as detailed invoices, trip reports or studies, exists to justify the expenses.**

- **Services paid for were used to improperly obtain, distribute or use information or data protected by law or regulation.**

- **Services paid for were intended to improperly influence the content of a solicitation, the evaluation of a proposal or quotation, the selection of sources for contract award or the negotiation of a contract, modification or claim. It does not matter whether the award is by the Government, a prime contractor or any tier subcontractor.**

- **Services paid for were obtained or performed in some way that violated a statute or regulation prohibiting improper business practices or conflict of interest.**

- **Services paid for violated a Federal, state or local statute or regulation.**

---

d. Certification of Indirect Costs

The Scenario

The auditor was assigned the task of performing a nomenclature review of the contractor's indirect cost submission for FY 1990, including a comparative analysis of the individual accounts to the prior year's audited account totals. Certain accounts showed percentage increases that warranted further audit. One account selected was Computer Expenses. In reviewing the charges to the account, the auditor discovered a significant amount for computer system hardware and software development. The auditor requested the supporting documentation for selected charges. The contractor provided project sheets and other documents to support ongoing small computer system upgrade and repair projects. Additionally, some of the expenses related to capitalization of system development costs. However, the documents did not cover all the project numbers and costs involved. Further research revealed that some of the expenses related to systems development work done in 1982 through 1986. The auditor reviewed the completed audit files for the contractor's 1982 through 1986 indirect cost submissions and found that the system development costs had been expensed during 1982 to 1986; however, the auditor had questioned some of the costs during the prior audits. In 1988, the Government and the contractor signed a written agreement as to how much of the costs would be reimbursed under Government contracts. The agreement covered the already incurred costs and an advance agreement as to the reimbursement of future costs. After the agreement, the contractor moved the agreed-to unreimbursable costs to a capital

Expenditure account. The capitalization schedule showed that the costs were to be written off over 5 years. The contractor representative could not explain the reason for including that cost in the FY 1990 submission. As part of the 1990 indirect cost submission, the contractor had included a signed Certificate of Indirect Cost as required by Defense Federal Acquisition Regulation Supplement (DFARS) 242.770-2.

General Comments. Effective March 12, 1985, contractors were required to certify that all costs included in a proposal to establish billing or final indirect cost rates are allowable in accordance with contract requirements and DoD cost principles. The certification must be submitted before the Government can accept the submission/proposal. In addition, for DoD cost-type and fixed-price incentive contracts in excess of $100,000 issued after February 26, 1987, the auditor should recommend penalties for claiming unallowable costs. The 10 U.S.C. 2324(a)-(d), implemented by DFARS 231.70, directs that penalties should be assessed if a contractor claims a cost in an indirect cost submission which is unallowable based on evidence that meets the clear and convincing standard for evidence. An unallowable cost that is judgment call or in a "gray area" will not satisfy the test.

This standard was revised by the 1993 DoD Authorization Act. The revised law applies to contractor fiscal years where an audit had not been formally initiated prior to October 23, 1992. The revised standard for assessing a penalty has been changed to "expressly unallowable under a FAR or DFAR cost principle that defines the allowability of specific costs. " The auditor must carefully evaluate each circumstance to determine if a fraud referral should be made.

FRAUD INDICATORS

Included in the indirect incurred cost submission:

- **expressly unallowable costs as specified in FAR 31.205 and/or Defense Federal Acquisition Regulation (DFAR) 15.205, which defines the allowability of specified selected costs;**

- **costs determined to be unallowable/nonreimbursable prior to the submission and specified as such in a written document, such as (1) a DCAA Form 1, "Notice of Contract Costs Suspended and/or Disapproved, " which was not appealed by the contractor or withdrawn by the DCAA, (2) a contracting officer determination or final opinion that was not appealed, or (3) a prior Armed Services Board of Contract Appeals or court decision involving the contractor, which upheld the cost disallowance;**

- **mutually agreed to unallowable costs, including directly associated costs. The mutual agreement must be in writing, specify, in detail, what costs are to be unallowable in the future and have occurred prior to the submission; or**

- **costs that were verbally agreed to or conceded to as unallowable if (1) the agreement occurred prior to the submission in question, (2) the process involved bidding rates, billing rates or a prior year's final indirect rates, and (3) the contractor changed the account that the cost were charged to in an apparent attempt to hid or conceal the costs.**

---

4. BILLING SYSTEMS AND RELATED REVIEWS

Government regulations allow for interim payment, if authorized, during contract performance. Payments can be through progress payments for fixed-price contracts or public vouchers for cost-type or time and material contracts. The contract will contain the appropriate clause which allows the interim payments and specifies the appropriate procedures, documents, etc. Public vouchers are normally submitted through the cognizant audit office for provisional approval prior to payment. In contrast, a contractor's progress payment request is reviewed by the audit office if the contracting officer requests it or if the auditor determines that it is in the best interests of the Government to do so. The primary objective of the review is to provide reasonable assurance that the amounts claimed are not more than what the contractor is allowed per the contract provisions. In addition, the contractor's billing system should be reviewed on a cyclical basis to determine the acceptability of the contractor's system and its procedures for preparation of reimbursement claims and progress payment requests.

Financial capability reviews can be performed for various reasons. Generally, during a progress payment review the auditor performs some assessment of the contractor's financial condition. The auditor should consider the contractor's financial condition when evaluating any fraud indicators found during an audit. Various financial situations may act as motivation for the contractor to commit fraudulent acts. Therefore, if a contractor is in poor or weak financial condition, the auditor should consider that additional audit steps may be necessary to protect the Government's interest.

Conversely, if the contractor has experienced a significantly higher profit on a contract than negotiated, the auditor should review the circumstances to determine if defective pricing may have occurred. Excess profits on either a specific contract, product line or division may be a fraud indicator. The auditor should carefully review the possible reasons for any excessive profits and consider them along with other fraud indicators when determining whether to make a referral.

a. Financing Inventory-Material Transfers

The Scenario

During a progress payment review, the auditor noted that the total material costs claimed on the progress payment under review had decreased from the material costs claimed on the prior request. The auditor further noted that the decrease resulted from an adjusting journal entry that transferred the material cost from the contract to other job orders. The auditor expanded the scope of the review and requested supporting documentation for the journal entries. The records showed which material costs had been transferred, the reason for the transfer and the responsible individuals. The journal entry explanation was "Material was transferred to work order number XXX." The charges were transferred from an ongoing contract to one just awarded. Additional questioning revealed that the new contract/work order was for a commercial contract. Interviews with responsible individuals-controller, program manager and material requisitioning manager-disclosed some important information:

-Contractor personnel knew about the impending award of a commercial contract when they ordered the material for the Government contract.

-Commercial and Government product lines are similar.

The company policy was to combine orders whenever possible to maximize savings. The company did not maintain an inventory except for small general use materials. Work orders were charged for material when received, not used. Since material was ordered on one purchase order, all the costs were charged to the existing open work order. Those costs, in turn, were billed to the Government through progress payments or public vouchers. The Government ended up paying the carrying and finance costs for the commercial job.

General Comments. Material cost transfers are always suspect. Auditors should review adjusting journal entries on a continuous basis and be alert for transfers significant in volume or cost. Most transfers will require additional information and supporting documentation before acceptance. In addition, the auditor should always be alert for billed costs that are not allocable or allowable on the contract. Cost transfers imply a breakdown in the accounting system-costs may not have been properly charged the first time. The contractor's accounting system must operate in an acceptable manner in order for the billing system to be acceptable.

FRAUD INDICATORS

- **Transfers from Government contracts to commercial contracts.**

- **Transfers to a "billable" contract or funding appropriation from one that cannot be billed on.**

- **Materials ordered and charged in excess of contract requirements.**

- **Initial billings for actual material costs far in excess of the negotiated material costs.**

- **Later billings showing a downward adjustment in material costs as labor/overhead costs increase.**

- **Transfers via any type of holding or suspense account.**

---

b.   Improper Billing of Costs

The Scenario

During a progress payment review, the auditor decided to verify billed material costs to actual invoices. The auditor judgmentally selected 10 of the larger dollar vendor charges for review and requested the supporting documentation including the original invoice, purchase order and shipping/receiving documents. The contractor was only able to produce copies of the vendor invoices. The auditor then sent confirmation letters to the various vendors to substantiate the charges. Two of the mailings were returned by the post office as undeliverable. Four of the vendors replied that their companies did not have any business with the contractor. The auditor also determined that two of the companies were closely held subsidiaries.

The auditor also attempted to review the estimate at completion calculation on the progress payment; however, the contractor had no supporting documentation. The auditor requested shipping documents to support the deliveries already made to the Government. None were available. Based on the delivery schedule in the contract and the percentage of costs incurred, the contractor should have made several shipments. The contractor stated that shipments had been made but no documents were available. The auditor also reviewed the contractor's float time for payment of vendor bills. The auditor checked the contractor's schedule for aging of payables back to the actual checks and invoices and found that the dates did not match the supporting documents. The contractor had altered both the invoice dates and the payment dates by one month. The adjustment made it appear that the contractor was paying its vendors within a month. In addition, the auditor also found some vendor invoices were not on the schedule. Those vendors had not been paid for over 120 days.

General Comments. Any audit that reviews a request for payment is sensitive. The auditor should always be aware of the contractor's financial condition. A weak financial condition may motivate the contractor to bill items improperly. In addition to reviewing the billed costs, the auditor must also review other calculations that impact the amount of costs reimbursed. Those include the estimate at completion, the cost of undelivered work, the liquidation rate and a flexible progress payment rate if applicable. Problems found in those situations should be further analyzed for possible referral.

FRAUD INDICATORS

- **Supporting documents missing or unavailable for review.**

- **Only copies of documents available for review.**

- **Slow in paying suppliers or nonpayments to suppliers. employees or Government.**

- **Billing costs that were not incurred on the contract.**

---

c. Total Contractor/Contract Environment

The Scenario

The auditor was assigned a progress payment to review. The contract involved was for a major weapon system and contained multiple funding appropriations. The administrative contracting officer (ACO) had only approved partial payment on the previous progress payment because all of the research and development (R&D) funds available on the contract had been billed. The auditor reviewed the incurred costs shown on the progress payment and noted that costs had been shifted from the R&D portion to the procurement portion of the contract. The auditor discussed the matter with the supervisor who explained that the contractor had decided to change how sustaining and nonsustaining engineering costs were defined and allocated. The auditor was informed that the contractor and the program office discussed the issue and it was under review. The auditor and the supervisor also discussed other deficiencies identified at the contractor location. A recent billing system review disclosed that the contractor had no policies and procedures for the calculation of the estimate at completion (EAC). However, the auditor found that the
EAC was based on an out-of-date delivery schedule. The contractor could not support the EAC calculation. Interviews of key personnel indicated that top management decreased component EACs without explanation. The contractor did not have budgets for indirect expense rates for the last 2 years. At the same time, the contractor was laying off employees and restructuring its management, but indirect rates continued to increase. The auditors also read several articles from financial publications that stated the corporation could experience financial difficulties depending on the outcome of certain events.

The auditor recommended that the ACO withhold an amount from the progress payment because of the unsupported EAC. The auditor also contacted the audit office cognizant of the corporate books and records to determine the overall financial condition of the company. Further discussions with the ACO determined that a subsequent progress payment had been made to the contractor at the insistence of the ACO's headquarters. The reason given was the company's pressing financial need. The auditor and the supervisor discussed the overall situation and decided to make a referral despite the implied Government acceptance of the contractor's actions.

General Comments. The auditor should consider the total contract/contractor environment when deciding whether to refer a suspected irregularity. While one indicator may not, in and of itself, be sufficient to warrant a referral, several seemingly unrelated deficiencies or indicators together may be more than enough. The auditor should not determine that a referral is inappropriate because of implied acceptance by Government officials of contractor actions. The key issue is whether the auditor would have referred the suspected irregularity if the Government official had not taken certain action. If the answer is yes, the auditor should still make the referral.

FRAUD INDICATORS

- Transfer of costs between various funding appropriations or other work orders that control the contractor's ability to be reimbursed.

- No supporting documentation for calculation of key figures, such as EACs or cost of undelivered work.

- The EACs for billing or contract performance reports differ from other internal financial EAC projections without reasonable explanations.

- Little or no physical progress even though significant costs have been billed and the contract delivery schedule indicates that significant physical progress should have occurred.

- Significant extensions to the contract delivery schedule with no increase in the EAC and the contractor has no acceptable explanation for why costs will not increase.

- Continued work performance problems identified by either the Government or the contractor, but no adjustments made to the EAC.

- The EAC calculated based on out-of-date delivery schedule.

- Billing for deliverables never received by the Government.

III. FORWARD PRICING PROPOSAL AUDITS

INTRODUCTION
Price proposals are submitted by the contractor in connection with the award, administration, modification or repricing of Government contracts or subcontracts when the contracting officer requires the submittal of cost or pricing data. The contracting office may then request an audit of the price proposal in accordance with FAR 15-805.5. Proposals may be based on cost estimates, incurred costs or any combination of the two. A proposal generally includes direct costs, such as material, labor, other direct costs or subcontracts and indirect costs. Many of the fraud indicators that may be identified during a proposal review are more noticeable during other types of audits, such as defective pricing reviews and incurred cost audits. Therefore, the auditor needs to be especially alert when reviewing proposals for possible fraud indicators.

1. ADJUSTMENT OF STANDARD COSTS

The Scenario

The auditor was assigned a proposal review at a contractor who generally bid on only a few fixed-price negotiated Government contracts that required the submittal of cost or pricing data. Most of the contractor's sales were to commercial companies or under competitively awarded Government contracts. Therefore, few fixed-price proposal audits were performed at the contractor each year and incurred cost audits were not applicable.

A standard cost system was used for material requirements and labor hours. The standards for labor hours were assigned by function (Fabrication, Assembly, Engineer and Quality Control) and labor classification (Levels 1 through 6). The labor quantity standards were based on "ideals," i.e., efficient performance under perfect conditions. The contractor calculated an average bid rate for each labor classification based on the current average labor hour rate and a company-wide average cost of living increase. The material requirements standards were established based on the raw material needed for the manufacture of each item. Those standards did not include any extra for scrap or inefficiencies in the manufacturing process. The material cost was bid using the estimated average cost for the existing bill of materials, which was based on the material requirements standards. Since the contractor had been manufacturing the items for several years, the labor and material standards had been set by an engineering study conducted several years ago.

In prior reviews, the auditor only performed a cursory review of the individual quantity standards. The auditor compared the proposed labor and material quantity standards proposed to those in the prior audit working papers and the contractor's computer run listing the individual standards. No exceptions were noted. No review of the variance allocation was performed. Since the standards were being used to bid quantities, the auditor qualified the proposal audit report because a technical evaluation was necessary to review the qualitative and quantitative aspects of the proposal.

For the current audit, the auditor requested the historical cost information for the last several contracts/work orders. The auditor then calculated the average unit historical cost and compared that to the proposed unit cost. The auditor determined the total proposed unit labor and material costs were within 5 percent of the historical unit cost for each of the selected work orders and functions. The auditor judgmentally selected some of the individual labor and material standards for review. The selected proposed standards were the same as the standards used to cost the prior contracts/work orders provided by the contractor.

The auditor tried to verify the calculation of the labor and material quantity variances. The variances were lumped into one account and spread equally among the various items produced. The auditor selected several units from the previous work history provided by the contractor and requested the routing slips for those units. In reviewing the routing slips, the auditor noted that unexplained additional labor hours and materials were added on the routing slip after the unit had passed quality control. The auditor then pulled a statistical sample of all the routing slips. In reviewing the selected routing slips to determine if the adding of extra hours and materials was "normal," the auditor found that units identified as commercial did not have the additional labor hours and material quantities added. The auditor also noted when tracing the costs to the books that the standards used on the commercial work were lower than those for the Government work.

General Comments. The key to identifying fraud indicators in a standard cost system is to understand the contractor's system-how the standards are developed; how, when and by whom the standards are updated; how the variance is allocated; and what weaknesses may exist in the internal control system. The auditor must also determine what types of standards the contractor uses. Standards can be classified as fixed or basic cost standards, theoretical or ideal standards or attainable standards. Fixed standards are used as a base to compare costs from year to year. Ideal standards are based on performance under perfect conditions. Ideal standards are often used to motivate program and functional managers to control costs.

Attainable standards are based on what reasonably can be achieved under current conditions. In addition, the allocation of variances over dissimilar product lines or contracts can be used to mischarge standard material costs. CAS 407, "Use of Stand3l.d Costs for Direct Material and Direct Labor," sets forth the requirements for using standard costs. The standard requires production units, defined as follows, for the use of standard costs:

> A group of activities which either has homogeneous inputs of direct material and direct labor or yields homogeneous outputs such that the costs or statistics related to these homogeneous inputs or outputs are appropriate as bases for allocating variances.

FRAUD INDICATORS

- High Efficiency (usage) variances.

- Seemingly unrelated task and steps on a statement of work, work breakdown structure, routing slip, description of work, etc.

- Efficiency (usage) standards are not updated over periods of time when the contractor recognizes and realizes improvements in the manufacturing technology or product design.

- Old, outdated standards are used to support proposals.

- The lack of a clear audit trail to verify the propriety of direct charges, such as labor, material and other direct costs.

- Weak internal controls that allow numerous opportunities to adjust direct charges, such as duplicate employee identification cards to charge labor hours on automated systems.

- Proposed standards for the same work differ based on the type of contract or work order the standards will be charged to. For example, lower standards used to charge commercial work versus negotiated Government contracts.

- Improper allocation of variances over dissimilar work.

2. LABOR CATEGORIES

The Scenario

The auditor was reviewing a contractor's proposal for a time and material (T&M) contract that had been awarded on a yearly basis for the last 2 years. Since the contractor involved had performed on the contract for the last 2 years, the auditor requested the incurred cost for the previous contracts and the year to date actual costs for the current ongoing effort. The auditor also specifically requested a breakdown of actual hours incurred by labor category and contract and the current employees identified by labor category.

The auditor compared the hours charged by labor category to those proposed. The auditor found that the contractor had charged about the same number of hours as proposed for each labor category. The auditor then computed the average historical hourly rate per category and compared it to the proposed rate. The auditor found that the incurred hourly rates were significantly lower than the proposed rates except for the administrative category. The auditor then reviewed the original proposal to determine the employees bid by labor category. The auditor found that the contractor did not have a full work force on board when the contract was originally bid. After being awarded the contract, the contractor was able to hire employees at lower salaries than proposed. The auditor asked the contractor why lower paid employees had been hired. The contractor representative responded that management knew at the time they bid the contract that lower paid employees could be hired to perform the work. The auditor then compared the qualifications of some of the newly hired employees with the requirements per the request for proposal. The auditor found that the contractor had placed many of the newly hired employees in labor categories for which they did not qualify.

General Comments. A T&M contract should be used to buy goods and services on the basis of direct labor hours at specified hourly rates that include wages, allocated indirect costs and profit, and materials at cost, including, if appropriate, material handling costs. A type of T&M contract is the labor hour contract. However, for a labor hour contract, the contractor does not supply materials. Those contracts should only be used when the Government cannot estimate, within reason: the work to be done; the period of performance; or the cost. Neither type of contract provides a positive profit incentive for the contractor to manage the labor force or control costs. Therefore, those contracts represent a higher risk area for the auditor and require greater surveillance.

FRAUD INDICATORS

- **Significant differences between proposed and actual unit costs or quantities with no corresponding changes in work scope or job requirements.**

- **Task-by-task billings consistently at the ceiling level established in the contract. An exception would be if the contract/work order specifies how many hours to bill.**

- **Specific individuals proposed as "key employees" not working on the contract.**

- **Proposed labor not based on existing work force. Massive new hires needed. New hire labor rates significantly lower than proposed.**

- **Employees' skills do not match the skill requirements as specified for their labor category or the contract requirements.**

- **Employees typically charged indirect by the company being charged direct to the contract.**

- **Partners', officers', supervisors' and other high level employees' time being charged in noncompliance with the contract terms or with the company's established accounting policies and procedures.**

- **Changes in the company's labor charging policies and procedures depending on the type of contract (fixed-price, cost-type, T&M or commercial).**

- **Repeated noncompliance with CAS 402, "Consistency in Allocating Cost Incurred for the Same Purpose, "for labor.**

---

3. FALSIFICATION OF DOCUMENTS

The Scenario

During a proposal review, the auditor was reviewing support for a proposed unit cost. The contractor had used actual cost as a basis for the proposal. The actual unit cost was supported by purchase order history. The auditor performed a statistical sample of the proposed bill of material and requested the supporting documentation for the selected items. The contractor provided copies of vendor invoices. The auditor closely reviewed the copies and noted some suspicious print type which did not match that of the rest of the invoice. The auditor expanded the review and requested the original invoice/document. On receiving the originals from the contractor, the auditor noted the following:

-The unit prices on the original invoices did not match the unit prices on the copies. Apparently, some had been altered by putting an additional number in front of the price or by moving decimals.

-Discount terms at the bottom of the invoice had been "whitened out" so the auditor would not notice an offered 20 percent discount.

General Comments. The auditor had performed a review of the purchasing system 2 years earlier. During that review, no significant deficiencies were noted. The auditor relied heavily on the results of that review and used only the purchase order history to verify unit prices. The contractor took advantage of the situation by altering selected invoices.

The auditor should periodically test the integrity of the accounting and operating systems he/she relies on. That can be done by doing transactional and compliance testing on a selected basis. In this case, it would involve requesting original documentation from the contractor to support the purchases order history. In other cases, the auditor may want to obtain third party confirmations from the actual vendors. The audit step might only be done on one or two transactions per proposal. The auditor could also randomly select a proposal and request the original documentation for a majority of the transactions. The auditor must be alert to changes in how a system works after he or she has reviewed and accepted it.

FRAUD INDICATORS

- **Original documentation consistently unavailable for the auditor's review.**

- **Consistently poor, illegible copies of supporting documentation.**

- **Different supporting documents provided for the same item with unit prices varying widely for the same part, for no obvious reason.**

- **Changes to the original documentation that do not appear to be authentic, such as different print or incorrect spacings.**

- **Information on the original document does not match information obtained from third party sources, such as confirmation letters to vendors/subcontractors or assist audits.**

---

4.   REPETITIVE BIDDING OF DUPLICATIVE MATERIAL COSTS

The Scenario

During the audit of a firm-fixed-price proposal, the auditor was reviewing the bill of materials when he/she noted that certain material/supplies were bid separately. The auditor did not remember seeing that type of material bid as a separate line on the "miscellaneous" bill of materials. The auditor reviewed the company's disclosed estimating practices and the disclosure statement which revealed that the company's normal practice was to bid that type of material, designated as abnormal supplies, as a percent factor applied to shop labor. The auditor discussed with the controller and estimating manager a possible noncompliance with CAS 402 and learned the following:

-Only supplies that become part of the end product were bid separately.

-The contractor's disclosed practice was to estimate "abnormal supplies," i.e., the cost of supplies that does not become a part of the end product by use of factor. That factor was calculated and applied to a base of shop labor costs.

-The contractor had established a part number code (XXX) labeled "abnormal supplies," and had begun to bid the item separately.

-The costs accumulated in part number code XXX were for "abnormal supplies," as described by the company's original policies.

-The auditor reviewed proposals that the contractor had submitted within the last year and confirmed the contractor repetitively bid "abnormal supplies" twice in each proposal-once as a separate item on the bill of materials and once as a factor.

General Comments. The auditor must know the contractor's disclosed estimating and accounting practices. Using that knowledge, the auditor can review proposed estimating or accounting changes and be alert for possible duplication of costs.

FRAUD INDICATORS:

- **Vague terms used to bid materials based solely on management's judgement or rough estimates.**

- **Repetitive noncompliance with the contractor's disclosed bidding/estimating practices.**

- **Repetitive, significant noncompliances with the CAS and/or the contractor's Disclosure Statement.**

---

5. EXCESS/RESIDUAL INVENTORY

The Scenario

The auditor was reviewing a proposal for the follow-on production of Lots 5 and 6. Lots 1 and 2 had been complete for 2 years, Lot 3 was just recently delivered, and Lot 4 was in production. Proposed material costs were based on actual costs for Lots 1 and 2. In reviewing the cost data for Lots 1, 2 and 3, the auditor found the following:

-Lots 1 and 2 showed material transferred to Lot 4 with no associated costs transferred.

-The actual costs per Lot 3 unit were less than the costs for Lots 1 and 2.

The auditor discussed the situation with the contractor's representative who provided additional information:

-The contractor had not yet reported excess material on Lots 1 and 2, even though the items were delivered 2 years ago.

-The proposed costs for Lots 3 and 4 were also based on the incurred costs for Lots 1 and 2.

-Extra material had been transferred from Lots 1 and 2 to Lot 4 production at no cost.

General Comments. Excess material is material that is acquired or furnished for a contract and not used or consumed during the performance of that contract. Title to excess contractor-purchased material belongs to the Government under completed cost-reimbursable contracts. Untimely transfer of excess inventory on either cost-type or fixed-price contracts affects the proposed costs for the next follow-on contract. When the contractor bases the proposed costs on historical costs, which include excess inventory, the cost of excess parts may be double-counted. Additional problems occur if the excess is then transferred to the follow-on job at no cost. Actual costs for the first job are overstated, while the actual costs for the follow-on job are understated.

FRAUD INDICATORS

- **No reporting of residual/excess materials.**

- **Transfers from prior lot work orders to current or forecasted work orders.**

- **Transfers from cost-type to fixed-price work orders.**

- **Transfers from cost-type to commercial work orders.**

- **Mass transfers to scrap accounts.**

- **Mass transfers to an inventory write-off account.**

- **Transfers to or via a suspense or any type of holding account.**

- **Poor internal controls over physical inventories.**

- **A disproportionate increase in the proposed scrap factor.**

- **A disproportionate increase in the inventory write-off account.**

- **Large quantity of or significant costs for "found" parts.**

III. FORWARD PRICING PROPOSAL AUDITS

IV. DEFECTIVE PRICING AUDITS

INTRODUCTION

The Truth In Negotiations Act, Public Law 87-653, gives the Government the right to adjust the contract price when it is based on inaccurate, incomplete or noncurrent cost or pricing data. Presently, DoD, National Aeronautics and Space Administration and Coast Guard contractors are required to certify that the data supplied to the Government are current, complete and accurate at the time of agreement on price for all negotiated procurements exceeding $500,000 unless the price is set by law or regulation, is based on adequate price competition, or is based on a vendor's established catalog or on the market price of commercial items sold in substantial quantities to the general public. On December 31, 1995, the 5-year period threshold ends and the threshold reverts back to $100,000 which had been the threshold since April 1, 1985. Defective pricing occurs when more current, complete and accurate data existed but were not disclosed to the Government, and the failure to disclose the data resulted in a significant increase in the contract price.

Auditors had not concentrated on finding indicators of defective pricing fraud until September 1983, when the DCAA provided its auditors a list of indicators as guides to determine when to make a referral. Those findings and conditions require further pursuit as potential cases of fraud are incorporated in the DCAA Contract Audit Manual, Chapter 14, Section 121, "Findings and Conditions Requiring Further Pursuit as Potential Cases of Fraud." From 1984 through 1992, DCAA reviewed 17,149 contracts and subcontracts, found 6,553 defectively priced and recommended contract prices be adjusted by over $7 billion. Of the 6,553 with recommended price reduction, 258 were referred for investigation. Auditors may need to more carefully consider fraud indicators when performing defective pricing reviews.

The following are general fraud indicators that relate directly to defective pricing reviews and should be considered for referral.

FRAUD INDICATORS

- High incidence of defective pricing.

- Repeated defective pricing involving similar patterns or conditions.

- Continued failure or refusal to correct known system deficiencies.

- Consistent failure to update cost or pricing data with knowledge that past activity showed that prices have decreased.

- Specific knowledge that is not disclosed regarding significant cost issues that will reduce the proposed cost.

- Repeated denial by responsible contractor employees of the existence of historical records that are subsequently found.

- Continued failure to make complete disclosure of data known to responsible personnel.

- Altered or false documents.

---

1. SELECTIVE DISCLOSURE

The Scenario

The auditor selected a Basic Ordering Agreement (BOA) for defective pricing review. Three recently placed orders under the BOA all exceeded $500,000 and were certified to by the contractor. The auditor requested the price negotiation memorandums (PNM) and reviewed the proposal audit files. The auditor performed an over and underrun analysis of costs bid versus costs incurred by element and found significant differences in labor. The auditor reviewed the PNM to obtain the basis for the agreement on hourly rates and labor hours. Further analysis showed the labor rates used at negotiations were the most current. However, the analysis showed a significant difference between the hours agreed to and the hours incurred.

The auditor reviewed the basis for the hours and found the contractor had selectively provided completed work orders to support the proposed labor hours. The auditor found that only a few of the work orders were provided for what appeared to be like items. The contractor representative stated that the work orders not provided were for different items. The work orders not provided showed lower hours for the completed work. The auditor contacted the Government technical representative and discussed the contractor's contention that the work orders not provided were for different items. The technical representative stated that not only were those the exact same items, but the contractor representative had previously written him stating the items were the same. The estimating deficiency was discussed with the contractor and an estimating system report was issued. The contractor agreed to correct the bidding procedure to include all appropriate work orders.

Later, the contractor negotiated an additional four work orders under the BOA. The auditor set up defective pricing reviews on each of the four new orders. Each exceeded $500,000 and was certified to by the contractor. The review of the PNM found the contractor again selectively disclosing the completed work orders showing the higher hours and not disclosing any of the work orders showing the lower hours, although they were to produce the same item.

The contractor agreed to correct the estimating system deficiency but failed to do so or to notify the Government prior to negotiations that the estimating procedure had not been corrected. Therefore, the auditor decided to make a referral.

General Comments. While the fraud indicators may be more likely to be found during a defective pricing review, the auditor may also find those indicators during an estimating system review.

FRAUD INDICATORS

- **Repeated defective pricing involving similar patterns or conditions.**

- **Continued failure to correct known system deficiencies.**

- **Failure to correct system deficiencies as agreed to by the contractor.**

- **Specific knowledge that is not disclosed regarding significant cost issues that will reduce the proposed cost.**

---

2. MANAGEMENT RESERVE

The Scenario

The auditor selected a contract for defective pricing review. The auditor obtained the proposal file and the PNM and discussed the negotiation with the contracting officer. A comparison between agreed-to and actual cost by element showed a significant underrun in labor cost. In trying to determine why the actual labor costs were so low, the auditor reviewed the contractor's process for determining the proposed hours and rates. The rates were found to be the most current information available at the time of negotiations.

The bid proposal stated that the hours were discretely estimated based on the engineer's analysis. When the estimate was presented to the engineer, the engineer indicated the hours seemed higher than his estimate. The engineer gave the auditor a copy of his original estimates. The auditor noted that the hours were less than the hours bid. The engineer had no idea why the hours had been increased.

The auditor had also started two other defective pricing reviews on negotiated awards for the same program. The auditor asked the same engineer responsible for the original estimate about the hours proposed on those contracts. The engineer stated that the proposed hours seemed excessive based on his company's internal management budget. The auditor received a copy of the contractor's internal management budget and the engineer's original budget and compared them. The internal management budget agreed with the engineer's original estimates. The auditor noted that the internal management budget documents had restrictive markings stating "Internal Use Only, Not Releasable to Government."

The auditor and Government technical representative talked to the contractor and were told that the difference between the proposed hours and the hours per the internal management budget/original engineering estimate represented a management reserve used to motivate its managers. The contractor responded that that was done on all contracts. The contractor could not explain how the difference was developed.

General Comments. Use of a management reserve is not in itself an improper management tool. However, management reserves should be established after costs are negotiated and should not affect the way costs are bid. The key is whether the data are disclosed in negotiating with the Government. The use of reserves to motivate employees may lead to increased susceptibility to fraud.

FRAUD INDICATORS

General

- **Proposal estimate, which was the basis for negotiation, is higher than supporting documentation with no creditable explanation.**

- **Contingencies are not disclosed.**

Defective Pricing

- **Knowledge that is not disclosed regarding significant cost issues that will reduce proposal costs.**

- **Continued failure to make complete disclosure of data known to responsible contractor personnel.**

---

3. COMBINING ITEMS

The Scenario

The auditor began a defective pricing review of a spare parts subcontract for a large weapon system. The prime contractor certified to the data and required the subcontractor to also certify. The auditor, during the detective pricing review, happened to read a subcontractor newsletter dated prior to negotiations, which mentioned a significant increase in spare parts sales. The newsletter mentioned six additional awards and how the subcontractor's backlog of orders would increase. The auditor remembered the PNM did not mention any other awards. The auditor reviewed the subcontractor's signed Standard Form 1411, "Contract Pricing Proposal Cover Sheet," and found a "NO" answer to item 12 which asked, "Have you been awarded any contracts or subcontracts for the same or similar items within the past 3 years?" Neither the Government nor the prime contractor was aware that the subcontractor negotiated six additional purchase orders for the same spare parts with different prime contractors on the day they were negotiating with the prime. Also, at the time of negotiation, the subcontractor had other subcontracts for the same spare parts but failed to disclose the costs.

The auditor obtained the actual costs by element and found significantly lower costs for material and labor. The auditor, remembering the newsletter, asked the subcontractor representative about the additional awards. The subcontractor representative stated that the additional awards were not the same. The auditor reviewed the bid file to obtain a list of the lower tier subcontractors and then requested the actual purchase orders. The purchase orders showed the quantity being purchased was six times as large as the subcontract being reviewed, but the price was 50 percent less than proposed.

The auditor contacted the contracting officers responsible for the six additional awards and confirmed that the spare part subcontracts were indeed for the same spare parts.

General Comments. Company publications or newsletters are good sources of information and audit leads on contractor operations. Subcontracts may be at higher risk for defective pricing because they were not properly reviewed during the proposal stage. The auditor must also remember that there are more parties involved in the process and, therefore, there are more opportunities for nondisclosure of information.

FRAUD INDICATORS

General
- **Cost estimates not based on total material requirements.**

- **Certification of false or misleading information**

Defective Pricing
- **Repeated defective pricing involving similar patterns or conditions.**

- **Specific knowledge that is not disclosed regarding significant cost issues that will reduce proposal costs.**

- **Continued failure to make complete disclosure of data known to responsible contractor personnel.**

---

4. MATERIAL AND SUBCONTRACT PRICING DEFICIENCIES

The Scenario

Audit management selected a large dollar fixed-price contract for a major weapon system for a defective pricing review. The contract contained a base production year with options for later year purchases. The auditor was assigned the material and subcontract costs for review. The auditor initially compared the actual costs incurred to the negotiated costs for the base year and found a significant cost difference. The auditor decided to review all 30 purchase orders/subcontracts that were over $10,000. The auditor compared the proposed/negotiated price of each purchase order/subcontract with the actual costs. As part of the review, the auditor also noted what company the original bid was based on versus which company the purchase order was issued to.

The auditor reviewed the purchase order/subcontract files to determine why different vendors were selected and why purchase orders were issued for lower costs than bid/negotiated. After reviewing vendor files, sending and receiving confirmation letters, obtaining the necessary assist audit reports and discussions with the contractor purchasing/subcontract management department, the auditor drew several conclusions. For two of the items, vendors bid were not the ones actually used. In one case, the confirmation letter revealed that the vendor had issued a "courtesy bid" when requested. The vendor stated that he/she never did business with the Government or a Government prime contractor because of all the red tape. In the second case, the confirmation letter to the vendor indicated that the vendor had sent a firm, written quote to the contractor that was substantially lower than the other vendor's quote. Even though the quote was issued several weeks prior to negotiations, the contractor used another vendor's higher quote to support the proposed costs at negotiations.

The auditor also identified four vendors who had originally submitted budgetary/planning quotes and later followed up with lower firm bids. The vendors stated the original request for quote sent out by the contractor only requested budgetary quotes. The contractor later requested "firm" quotes from the vendors who bid lower. However, the contractor used the higher budgetary quotes to support the proposed costs. The remaining four subcontracts reviewed were sole source awards. The auditor found that the files were poorly documented. The sole source justifications were not adequate. The contractor did not perform any market search for alternative sources. The auditor requested assist audits on the four subcontracts. The auditors who performed the assist audits had similar documentation problems. The agreement on price date was not documented. There was little supporting documentation for the proposed costs. The subcontract auditors noted that the subcontractors' indirect rates included significant amounts for business meals and entertainment. The auditors found that the subcontractors' salesmen were buying the contractor's subcontract buyers frequent luncheons and dinners. The assist audit reports indicated that the subcontract prices had been partially negotiated prior to the contractor's negotiations with the Government. The subcontract negotiations had already provided for a 25-percentreduction, about which the contractor failed to inform the Government negotiator.

General Comments. An effective audit technique that has been used to validate the completeness, accuracy and currency of the prime contractor's proposed subcontract/vendor prices is to "mail out" inquiries to companies shown on the prime's bidder mailing lists. The procedure has proven successful in that it identifies lower bids received but not documented in the contractor's purchasing files. Confirmation letters may also provide information which indicates the existence of a kickback or bribery scheme.

FRAUD INDICATORS

General

- A significant variance between proposed and negotiated vendor/ subcontract prices.

- High percentage of sole source (noncompetitive) subcontract awards with poor explanations/documentation.

- Contractor using higher budgetary/planning quote to support proposal or negotiations knowing that a lower firm quote has been or will be submitted on request.

- Contractor using higher courtesy bids to support proposal or negotiations knowing that lower bids are or will be available. Courtesy bids also increase the lowest bid.

- Failure to disclose the existence of a decrement factor or historical negotiation experience with vendors.

- Failure to disclose decreases in subcontract pricings even though some parts of the subcontracts are still under negotiation.

- Pattern of subcontractor employees buying contractor employees lunches, dinners and/or other items. Individual items may be of low value, but the aggregate value of all items is fairly material.

Defective Pricing

- Specific knowledge that is not disclosed regarding significant cost issues that will reduce the proposed cost.

- Continued failure to make complete disclosure of data known to responsible personnel.

---

5. CHANGING FROM MAKE TO BUY

The Scenario

The auditor began a defective pricing review on a contract for $1 million. One of the auditor's first review steps was to compare the proposed costs to the actual incurred costs by examining each cost element, such as labor, material, subcontracts and other direct costs. The auditor noticed a significant difference between the proposed and actual incurred costs for materials. It was important to obtain the PNM and proposal to determine exactly what was proposed and when. A further check showed that the company proposed to make the item in-house but, in fact, purchased it from an outside vendor at a significantly lower price. When the auditor questioned the subcontract manager, she stated that they have been making the item for years, but the records may be hard to locate.

The auditor contacted the vendor that supplied the items and requested confirmation of when discussions occurred with the company about supplying the items. The supplier stated that he "faxed" his price 2 weeks prior to negotiations and also noted that he has supplied the same items for prior contracts.

The auditor next reviewed other contracts and found the items were indeed provided as the supplier stated. The file included the "fax" with a date after the agreement on price date. However, the date appeared to have been changed or altered. The copy the auditor received from the supplier showed the date of 2 weeks before the contract price between the company and the Government was reached. When the auditor reviewed the estimating system survey report, he/she noticed that the contractor's estimating system had as a deficiency in the prior comprehensive report and flash estimating system deficiency reports the condition of proposing an item as being made in-house and later reversing to buy. The reversion seemed to occur within 2 weeks of price agreements on the last five major buys.

After discussing the nondisclosure with the contractor, the contractor submitted a certified offset that effectively negated the amount of the auditor's recommended price adjustment. Since the auditor had not found any additional recommended price adjustments, a negative defective pricing audit report was prepared. The auditor discussed the make versus buy change with the supervisor to determine if it should be referred. Because of the nature of the audit finding, the auditor and supervisor agreed to make the referral.

General Comments. Switching from make to buy or vice versa should be considered a fraud indicator if the contractor experiences lower costs from the change in methods. A pattern of switching is a definite fraud indicator. The contractor may have failed to disclose a planned change prior to negotiation or may have a history of switching after negotiations.

FRAUD INDICATORS

- **Pattern of switching from make to buy or vice versa without proper notification to the Government.**

- **Documented lower vendor price and still proposing as a make item.**

- **Indications of altered supporting document.**

- **Continued failure to correct known system deficiencies.**

---

6. OTHER FRAUD INDICATORS

In the previous scenarios we have described various fraud indicators that auditors may find during defective pricing reviews or in other audits. Below are some additional fraud indicators that the auditor may encounter during any type audit:

   -Intentionally duplicating/double counting costs by proposing or claiming them as direct and indirect.

   -Proposing obsolete/unnecessary items.

   -Including in proposals or claims inflated rates for items, such as insurance or workmen's compensation.

-Purging proposal files of documents showing other vendors with lower prices than the vendor selected.

-Failing to disclose excess inventory that is used on later contracts.

-Refusing to provide requested data which show lower costs.

-Planning to use an intercompany division to perform part of contract but proposing an outside vendor or another division. Also can be the opposite way.

-Suppressing internal/external studies or reports which may affect proposed costs, i.e., more efficient equipment, manufacturing processes, etc.

-Commingling work orders to hide productivity improvements.

-Withholding information on batch purchases.

-Failing to disclose internal documents on discounts.

APPENDIX

**DCAA FORM 2000.0, SUSPECTED IRREGULARITY
REFERRAL FORM, SEPTEMBER 1991**

THIS FORM NOT AVAILABLE IN TEXT FORMAT.
AVAILABLE IN PDF VERSION.